Canada

Canada is the second largest country in the world. It covers an area of nearly ten million square kilometres yet its population is less than half that of Great Britain. This vast and empty land contains some of the most beautiful and rugged scenery in the world. The Rocky Mountains of British Columbia and Alberta rise to 6,050 metres while the Great Lakes of Ontario comprise the largest area of freshwater lakes anywhere in the world.

Canada has extremes of climate which vary from frozen desert in the north to temperate in the south-west. It is also a land rich in natural resources – coal, oil gold, copper and nickel and others waiting to be developed.

The Canadians are hardy people, fiercely proud of their beautiful country. Jack Brickenden, who lives in Toronto, is a freelance radio, TV and newspaper journalist. He has travelled extensively throughout his homeland in the preparation of this book.

ARCTIC OCEAN
GREENLAND
ALASKA
Inuvik
Arctic Circle
Ft. Selkirk
Whitehorse
YUKON TERRITORY
Rocky Mountains
NORTHWEST TERRITORIES
NEWFOUNDLAND
Hudson Bay
Labrador
BRITISH COLUMBIA
ALBERTA
SASKATCHEWAN
MANITOBA
QUEBEC
Edmonton
Banff
Calgary
Vancouver Island
Vancouver
PACIFIC OCEAN
ONTARIO
PRINCE EDWARD ISLAND
NEW BRUNSWICK
Regina
Cardale
Quebec
Ste. Marie Among the Hurons
Halifax
NOVA SCOTIA
Montreal
Hull
L. Superior
Sudbury
Ottawa
St. Lawrence Seaway
L. Huron
Algonquin Park
Georgian Bay
Collingwood
Toronto
L. Ontario
Great Lakes
Niagara Falls
Welland Canal
L. Erie
USA
ATLANTIC OCEAN

we live in CANADA

Jack Brickenden

Wayland

Living Here

We live in Argentina
We live in Australia
We live in Brazil
We live in Britain
We live in Canada
We live in the Caribbean
We live in Chile
We live in China
We live in Denmark
We live in France
We live in Greece
We live in India
We live in Israel
We live in Italy

We live in Japan
We live in Kenya
We live in Malaysia and Singapore
We live in Mexico
We live in New Zealand
We live in Pakistan
We live in Poland
We live in South Africa
We live in Spain
We live in Sweden
We live in the U.S.A.
We live in the Asian U.S.S.R.
We live in the European U.S.S.R.
We live in West Germany

The author and publishers would like to acknowledge with thanks the kind help of Canadian Pacific Airlines who provided the author with free transport around Canada.

First published in 1984 by
Wayland (Publishers) Ltd
49 Lansdowne Place, Hove
East Sussex BN3 1HF, England

© Copyright 1984 Wayland (Publishers) Ltd

ISBN 0 85340 856 4

Phototypeset by Kalligraphics Ltd
Redhill, Surrey
Printed in Italy by G. Canale & C.S.p.A., Turin
Bound in the U.K. by The Pitman Press, Bath

Contents

Jerome Ber'ube, *trip leader* — 6
Peter Green, *Inuit spokesman* — 8
Doug Wootton, *trapper* — 10
Bill Liddell, *cruise ship captain* — 12
Jack McDonald, *railroad conductor* — 14
Peggy Longstaff, *prairie farmer* — 16
Malcolm Campbell, *St. Lawrence Seaway official* — 18
Cyril Harnish, *lobster fisherman* — 20
Art Elmhirst, *bush pilot* — 22
Sharon Armstrong, *keeper of historic site* — 24
Monica Lacock, *CN Tower hostess* — 26
Ron Tozer, *park naturalist* — 28
Pat Cummins, *oil company geologist* — 30
Jacquelyn Fraser, *schoolgirl* — 32
John Crosbie, *MP* — 34
Dave Ridgeway, *Canadian footballer* — 36
Robin Rose, *miner* — 38
Ian MacDonald, *mountie* — 40
Ron Harthill, *logger* — 42
Robert MacLean, *chef* — 44
Francine Letellier, *librarian* — 46
Peter Allchin, *airline company director* — 48
Gordon Byce, *Indian counsellor and clergyman* — 50
Jane McNulty, *teacher* — 52
Bob Burt, *radio producer* — 54
Teresa Proskurniak, *dancer* — 56
Facts — 58
Glossary — 59
Index — 60

'I am a big fan of nature'

Jerome Ber'ube is 22 and a Quebec-born Canadian whose home is in Montreal but who works in English Canada. He is a trip leader on the big rubber rafts that take adventurers through the turbulent whitewater rapids of the mighty Ottawa River.

I do seasonal work — all outdoors. In the summer I work on the Ottawa River in the whitewater rafting business. In winter I am a ski instructor. I am not interested in doing one job all the year round.

The Ottawa River is about 120 kilometres (75 miles) west of our national capital, Ottawa. It flows between the provinces of Quebec and Ontario and empties

Jerome explains some of the dangers of whitewater rafting before a new crew sets out on the Ottawa River.

into the great St. Lawrence River, which in turn empties into the Atlantic Ocean. During the early fur-trading days the Ottawa River was one of the main canoe routes into the Canadian interior. Here the river runs wild through many islands. It is a world class waterway with rolling waves and boiling, cascading water chutes. We take people over the rapids in big, sixteen-passenger rubber rafts. The waves are like huge roller coasters. My job as trip leader is to steer the boat through the rapids for the most excitement and the least risk.

You can't steer a craft unless it is moving forward in the water, no matter how fast the current is moving by itself. To control a raft the people on board must paddle hard so I can steer and keep us safe as we ride the hydraulics down the river. The people pay to come down the river with us but they still have to paddle.

The whitewater rafting company is called Wilderness Tours and it also runs river tours in Quebec Province and New York State. It began operating on the

Shooting the rapids in a Wilderness Tours rubber raft.

Ottawa River in 1975 and has rafted nearly 90,000 people from all over the world through the rapids. We have never had a serious accident.

I guess I am a big fan of nature. In late winter or early spring, when the skiing is over and the whitewater rafting has not yet begun, I take my bike and go into the back country of Quebec. This is the time of year we harvest the maple syrup. In English it is called 'sugaring off'. The mature maple trees, the ones called hard maples or sugar maples, are tapped by driving a spigot into the tree with a bucket or plastic tube attached to collect the sap. In the spring with warm days and cold nights the maple sap moves up from the roots of the tree to bring life back into the tree. This is the syrup. You can taste it as it oozes to the surface of the bark. It is sweet, but it is very thin. To make 4½ litres (one gallon) of maple syrup you have to collect 180 litres (40 gallons) of sap from the trees. This sap is placed in huge vats and a fire is kept burning underneath until the sap has thickened enough to be maple syrup.

It is handled quite scientifically now in most areas, but in the backwoods in the old days, and sometimes even today, the rendering of the sap is done outdoors in the snow and it is a great social event. People from neighbouring farms or villages gather around for the 'sugaring off', to sample the syrup and to make what we call sugar-on-snow. To do this you splash some of the hot, thickened sap on to clean snow on the ground. The cold immediately turns the sap to toffee and you can pick the maple candy out of the snow and chew it. It is a great delicacy among the people of Quebec.

7

'They are looking for ways to divide us'

The Inuvialuit people live in Canada's western Arctic. They still hunt and fish but their lives are changing under the white man's influence. Peter Green speaks for his people in their negotiations for native rights. He is 39 and lives in Inuvik in the Northwest Territories.

Tuktoyaktuk, Inuvik, Sachs Harbour, Aklavik, Paulatuk and Holman Island are the six communities in the western Arctic where the Inuvialuit people live. There are about 2,500 native people in this area. They are all members of a larger group of people called Inuit. We used to be called Eskimos, but that is an Indian word not our own. Inuit simply means 'the people'.

I am chairman of COPE, the Committee for Original Peoples' Entitlement. This is an organization founded in Inuvik, in the Northwest Territories. It provides a united voice for the original peoples of this region and works for their rights. We are under a lot of pressure right now. There is oil and gas development in the Arctic and this threatens our way of life and our rights to the land on which we depend.

The Inuvialuit people are primarily hunters and fishermen. I suppose that about eighty per cent of my diet consists of caribou meat. The remainder is fish. We can buy vegetables, though, from the Hudson's Bay store in Inuvik.

Nowadays, the most common form of transport used by the Inuit is the snowmobile.

To live in the Arctic demands strength and skill. We exhibit these in our traditional sports. They are generations old and still continue to test the men and women who live in this region. The games include high kicks, canoe races, kneel-and-jump, tug-of-war, blanket toss (where a person is thrown high in the air by other people holding the sides of a blanket), and the good woman events. These include such things as bannock baking, tea boiling and goose plucking.

Here, the sun goes down in December and that's the last you see of it until February. In summer, when the ice on seas, rivers and lakes has melted, the Inuvialuit use boats to travel around in search of the animals and fish they hunt. In winter dog teams or power sleds are used. I have made a few trips of 130 or 150 kilometres (80 or 90 miles) by dog team using seven or eight dogs harnessed singly or in pairs. When I can I like to fish for Arctic char or hunt caribou and duck. But most of my time now is spent working for COPE. It isn't my choice to be always going south lobbying and negotiating on behalf of my people but it has to be done. I can only go hunting for about thirty days a year now; the rest of the time I spend dealing with the Canadian government trying to protect the rights of the Inuvialuit.

It is only by speaking with one voice that we can stand against those who devour our lands. We are like the caribou when the hungry wolves come. They are looking for ways to divide us, to make us run in different directions so that we are easier prey. I am fighting that.

Peter occasionally finds time to harness up the dogs and take off on a hunting expedition.

'The whisky froze solid. It was sixty below zero'

Doug Wootton is a fur trapper in the winter and he sluices for gold in the summer. His trapline is about 480 kilometres (300 miles) from the Arctic Circle in Canada's Yukon Territory. He sets traps for lynx, marten and fox.

I trap about 480 kilometres (300 miles) south of the Arctic Circle where the Yukon River meets the Pelly. We call it the Fort Selkirk area after a trading post that had been built here about 150 years ago. It's a ghost town now. Because I'm a white man I can't own a trapline. This is a government regulation to protect the Indians. So I work in partnership with Danny Roberts. He is a native and very superstitious. There are places in the bush that he won't go to.

The trapping season starts in early November and ends late in May. This is the time of year when an animal's fur gets thicker and fetches a better price. There's a wide variety of animals up here but I trap for lynx, marten and fox. I don't touch the wolverine, though; he's too smart for me. He'll spring the trap and eat the bait.

When I lay out my traps I travel up to 19 kilometres (12 miles) from Fort Selkirk by snow machine. Then I trudge another 11 kilometres (7 miles) or so on snowshoes. I watch for the narrow parts on a trail where animals might have to pass, or I watch for animal signs: that's where I set my traps.

I hollow out a place in the snow and set the baited trap in the hollow. Then I use my snow paddle to break up the snow real fine and draw it over the trap so there's no disturbance on the surface. I chain the trap

Doug setting his trap. It is chained to a tree to prevent the animal escaping.

Doug and his Indian partner, Danny Roberts, examine furs outside their log cabin.

to a tree, under the snow, and then smear bait on the tree to attract the animal's attention. Then I go back to my cabin for a few days. I set about fifteen or twenty traps a day and visit them to take the catch and reset the traps about every four days.

This can be rough country up here. One winter I was trapped in my cabin because the river hadn't frozen over enough for me to cross. I nearly starved to death. The whisky in my bottle froze solid. It was sixty degrees below zero centigrade (minus eighty degrees fahrenheit).

In summer, though, it's as warm as Hawaii up here. There's no trapping then so I go after gold. There's still gold in the Yukon. I sluice for mine. During the famous gold rush days of the Klondike, there were 50,000 people up around Dawson City going wild for gold. Today it has a population of about 500.

I look for what we call 'flour gold' – tiny, powdery fragments of gold that have been ground down by the normal movements of the earth. I wash silt-laden water through my sluice boxes and take the fine gold powder out when it sticks to the mercury-coated copper plates in the box. Then I remove the gold from the mercury. Some seasons I get up to 850 grams (30 ounces) At today's prices that's worth about $10,000. It won't make my fortune but it's enough for me.

11

'The best-known holiday area in the world'

Bill Liddell is captain of the cruise ship *Maid of the Mist IV*, one of four sturdy little vessels that carry their passengers right into the foaming spray of that massive wonder of the world, Niagara Falls.

There is an ancient legend about a beautiful Indian princess named Lelawala, daughter of Chief Eagle Eye, who went over Niagara Falls in a white birch-bark canoe as a sacrifice to appease the gods. She died in the falls but her ghost lived on in the caves below the cataract as the 'Maid of the Mist'.

That's where the name came from for

Captain Liddell and his passengers approaching Horseshoe Falls.

the little cruise ships we use to carry visitors to the base of Niagara Falls — within 68 metres (75 yards) of the point where the water from Canada's Horseshoe Falls roars into the river. The spray from the falls is so heavy that all the passengers have to wear black raincoats and hats.

I am captain of *Maid of the Mist IV*, which is the largest ship of the four operated by the Maid of the Mist Company. She is 22 metres (72 feet) long and 7 metres (24 feet) broad and carries 200 passengers. The first *Maid of the Mist* was a steamboat that was launched in the Niagara River in 1846. In the long history of these sturdy little boats no engine has ever failed nor has there ever been an accident.

An estimated 14 million people visit Niagara Falls each year and of these about 500,000 take the trip aboard the *Maid of the Mist*. It's only a 3.2-kilometre (two-mile) round trip from the docking area, past the American Falls, and up into the foaming spray of Canada's Horseshoe Falls. Ninety per cent of all the water that goes over Niagara passes over the Canadian side. I think when the international boundary was drawn down the middle of the Niagara River Canada got the better end of the deal.

Niagara Falls has been described as the best known holiday area in the world. I don't know whether this is true but people come from all over the world to see the falls. On our boats we have tourists from France, Germany, Japan, Italy, Puerto Rico, various South American countries, Switzerland, Britain, and Australia; and of course there are many Canadians and Americans.

The reason Niagara Falls is there is because of a fault – a geological fault called the Niagara Escarpment. This is a huge ridge of land that stretches 320 kilometres (200 miles) north west from the Niagara Peninsula. At Niagara the water going over the falls drops 54 metres (176 feet) straight down into the deep water.

The Niagara River is only 56 kilometres (35 miles) long. It connects Lake Erie with Lake Ontario and in order to bring shipping into and out of the Great Lakes it was necessary to build eight locks to get around Niagara Falls. At one time – 12,000 years ago – the falls were eleven kilometres (seven miles) downstream, but the endless pounding and wear and tear of the water very gradually wore away the lip of the falls so that it worked its way up river to its present location. The present estimate is that Niagara Falls is eroding, or moving back, at the rate of about 0.3 metres (one foot) in ten years, so it'll still be there if you want to come and look.

The Maid of the Mist IV *sailing into the foaming waters of Niagara Falls.*

'Freight trains have as many as 150 cars'

Jack McDonald is a conductor on the Canadian Pacific Railway. This is the rail system that was created so that Canada could become one country. It was the vital link across northern North America that made Canadian development possible.

The story of the Canadian Pacific Railway (CPR) and the history of Canada are the warp and weft of the creation of Canada as a nation. More than any other enterprise in Canada, with the possible exception of the Hudson's Bay Company, CPR was instrumental in forming the destiny and future of this nation. Canada became a confederation in 1867. This was nearly a century after our dynamic and rapidly growing neighbour to the south had achieved her own independence. At that time there were very few railway lines in Canada and all of them were in the east. The total population of the new nation was only 4,000,000. In the United States the population was already ten times that total.

The Dominion of Canada was made up of only four provinces at that time: Nova Scotia, New Brunswick, Quebec and Ontario. To the west stretched thousands

Jack's trans-Canada passenger train pulls into Banff Station in the Rockies.

A Canadian Pacific Railways freight train winds its way through the mountains.

of kilometres of sparsely populated prairie and mountain regions connected only by wagon trail, steamer or canoe routes to the rest of the dominion. There had been concern for years about political pressure from the United States causing expansion northwards into Canadian territory: Canadians feared that their country might be annexed. If they as a nation were to become strong, united and progressive there had to be a tangible link between the Atlantic provinces and the Pacific Ocean — a railway. And so the Canadian Pacific Railway Company was created in 1881. The last spike in the CPR trans-continental railway was driven at Craigellachie, in British Columbia, on 7th November 1885. Within six months the first passenger train, the *Pacific Express*, left Montreal on Monday evening and arrived in Port Moody in British Columbia, on schedule, at noon on the following Sunday, 139 hours later.

I am a conductor on the passenger train travelling through the Rocky Mountains from Calgary to Vancouver, on the Pacific Ocean. A passenger train in Canada might have ten or a dozen cars. A freight train can have as many as 150 cars. It is strange and exciting, going through the Rockies, to see your freight train coming out of one of the famous spiral tunnels of the Kicking Horse Pass while the tail end is still going in at the start of the tunnel. These two tunnels are about 900 metres (3,000 feet) long and were built in order to overcome a dangerously steep grade between Banff and the town of Field high in the mountains. It took 1,000 men two years to complete the construction of these two tunnels.

CPR's main business on the railway now is freight. Passenger service is handled through a co-operative arrangement called VIARail which uses both CPR and Canadian National Railways crews. On the freight side, CPR carries wheat and other grains, coal, potash, sulphur, copper and nickel ores, sand and stone, container traffic, forest products, liquid petroleum gas, gypsum, iron ore, oil, gas, chemicals, and phosphate rock. We operate over 27,000 kilometres (16,700 miles) of track throughout Canada.

A lot of people live in Canada today because of the railroad. The CPR became involved in an extensive colonization programme once the railroad was completed, and also thousands upon thousands of people who came to Canada from all over the world to work on the railroad stayed on to become citizens. There were Poles, Ukrainians, Chinese and many others.

I'm retiring in a few years. My plan for the future is to travel by train wherever and as far as I can. I love the railroad.

'Occupied farmland exceeds 68 million hectares'

Peggy Longstaff, her husband William, and their three sons are wheat farmers in Cardale, Manitoba, the eastern extremity of the great Canadian prairies. The Longstaffs farm about 1,300 hectares (five square miles) of prairie land. The family has been working this land since 1911.

We farm as a family. On our farm three of our sons are farming, along with ourselves. Each has his own portion of the land. Wheat is our main crop, but we grow barley if the price is right and the boys like to grow flax. The choice of what crop to grow changes according to world demand. Our big acreage has been wheat over the last few years, but we've had some dry seasons. One year we had a dry spring and had to re-seed a lot of the crop because it didn't germinate. But we don't get discouraged. There's always next year.

Agriculture is the main primary industry in Canada, and we usually hold one-third of the world wheat export market, sharing it with the United States, Australia and Argentina. Occupied farm land in Canada exceeds 68 million hectares (170 million acres). Most of the wheat is grown in Manitoba, Saskatchewan and Alberta. The great plains of North America are called the prairies here in Canada. They start about 72 kilometres (45 miles) south of here and spread and expand west and north across the three prairie provinces. This wheat growing area is almost 1,600 kilometres (1,000 miles) from east to west.

There weren't many trees here until the land was settled. That surprised me. When I came here in the forties I thought of it as a forested country. But the trees didn't come until farming had been started. This particular part of the prairies is called pothole country. There are lots of little sloughs (pronounced 'sloos') surrounded by trees

Peggy sweeps the porch of the family's wooden farmstead.

that cut down on the amount of arable land. We can only use about seventy-five per cent of the land we own. A slough is a depression in the ground that fills up with water in the spring from melting snow. You can't use it because it never dries up except in periods of drought. The sloughs are teeming with wild duck and other wildlife. My son saw fifteen or sixteen deer one morning in front of our house. They had come from the sloughs.

In Canada you market your wheat through the government Wheat Board, which is the only selling agency for export grain. The farmer delivers his crop to the co-operative which is made up from the farmers in the region. The price is set at the beginning of the crop year, so we know in advance what we are going to get. If the Wheat Board sells it for more, then there is an additional payment to the members of the co-op. We know far enough in advance what is worth raising that year and what isn't, so there's no great gamble. The real gamble is nature. Last year barley was a very poor crop, but this year since the American corn crop has suffered a lot of damage the price of barley has gone up.

We belong to a religious group called The Brethren. In Canada 45 per cent of the population is Roman Catholic; 20 per cent are United Church; 13 per cent are Anglican (which used to be known as Church of England in Canada), and there are Presbyterians, Methodists, Baptists and some others. The Brethren is a small denomination that doesn't believe in having a pastor or a minister. Every man in the congregation is responsible for the service. The Brethren came from England originally, where they were known as the Plymouth Brethren. We just like to call ourselves The Brethren.

The Canadian prairies are 1,600 kilometres (1,000 miles) of flat farming country.

'It's Canada's fourth seacoast'

Malcolm Campbell runs Canada's Welland Canal system, part of the vast inland waterway that lifts huge ocean-going vessels a total of 180 metres (600 feet) as they pass through the mighty St. Lawrence Seaway.

When I talk about how big everything is in Canada I'm not boasting. I am talking about a way of life. Distance and size dictate our lifestyle in this country. Cities are hundreds of kilometres apart. Everything is big. The lakes are the biggest, the prairies are the biggest, the tundra, the coastline, the mountain ranges, the geographical variety – all are extreme.

This great size is well represented in our

The St. Lawrence Seaway is over 3,700 kilometres (2,300 miles) long and connects the Great Lakes with the Atlantic Ocean.

inland waterway where I work. It is often referred to as Canada's fourth seacoast. We have the Atlantic coast, the Pacific coast, the Arctic coast, and we also have an inland 'seacoast' that stretches more than 3,700 kilometres (2,300 miles) into the heart of North America. This is the St. Lawrence Seaway which comprises all the Great Lakes – Lake Superior, Lake Michigan, Lake Huron and Georgian Bay, Lake St. Clair, Lake Erie, Lake Ontario plus the St. Lawrence River and all the other rivers that connect these enormous freshwater lakes. I am in charge of the Welland Canal system which carries ships past the Niagara Escarpment and Niagara Falls.

Traditionally, the economy of most countries dictates that the coastal area is the dominating region. It has always been so. In North America it is the interior that dominates in agriculture, industrial production, population and employment. For Canada and the United States that powerful interior industrial region is reached through the St. Lawrence Seaway. Ocean vessels enter the inland waterway through the Gulf of St. Lawrence and the St. Lawrence River. Once the ship has reached the western end of Lake Superior, at the other end of the seaway, she has travelled more than 3,700 kilometres (2,300 miles) inland and climbed more than 180 metres (600 feet) above sea level.

Canada and the United States operate the seaway jointly. Under the present arrangement neither nation could operate it independently. We work together. There are fifteen locks in the system. Seven are on the St. Lawrence River and of these two are American. There are eight here at Welland, all of which are Canadian. There are also four main locks at Sault Ste. Marie, Michigan, which connect with Lake Superior, run by the Americans. The locks

The Welland Canal system carries ships past the Niagara Falls.

on both sides of the international boundary are fitted out the same way and run the same way – user pays. This means that if you want to bring your ship through the seaway you pay for this service according to your tonnage.

Every spring when the first ship comes into harbour off the lake, either upstream or down, we present the skipper with a traditional top hat. There is a great fuss – an official presentation, news coverage, the mayor making a speech. But the captain doesn't get to keep the top hat. He signs its brim and hands it back for us to keep for further presentation the next spring. The captain, however, does get a gift certificate at a local haberdasher so he can buy a hat for himself. This year a Swedish ship was first in harbour. The captain loved the whole idea of the symbolic topper and invited everyone to come aboard and have a little celebration. He really got into the spirit of the thing.

'A hundred thousand welcomes'

Cyril Harnish is a lobster fisherman in Nova Scotia. For all his seventy years he has lived within sight of the Atlantic Ocean. For fifty of those years he has fished for lobster. He has never been outside Canada's maritime provinces and he is a happy man.

Prince Edward Island and Nova Scotia are the main lobster fishing grounds in Canada. I've lived here all my life, and since I left school I've spent all my time fishing. I've gone after mackerel, cod, pollock and herring, but mostly I've fished for lobster. Canada is famous for its lobsters.

Nova Scotia is famous for its lobsters. This fishing village is littered with pots for catching them.

They sell all over the world. Maybe some of mine are selling in Europe right now.

During the season I load my boat each morning and go to set my gear out at eight o'clock. For lobster, I can set my traps close to shore, where the bottom is rocky. A lobster trap or 'pot' is a wooden frame covered by netting. It lets the lobster in after the bait you set for him, but once he's in, he can't get out again.

I go back the next day to haul in the traps. Sometimes I get up to eight lobsters in one trap. I have to be careful when I get them out because their claws are very powerful and you can easily lose a finger. Usually they weigh between 0.5 kilograms and 1.5 kilograms (1–3 pounds). I sell them down the road at Shatford's Lobster Pound for about $7.20 a kilo ($3.30 a pound). That's a fair price.

The smallest lobster you can legally keep is a pound (0.45 kilograms). If they're less than that I have to throw them back. The biggest I ever caught weighed 9.5 kilograms (21 pounds). That one was no good

Halifax is the capital of Nova Scotia and one of the main ports on Canada's east coast.

for eating though. It was too old and tough. There's a big one up at the Clearwater Pound near Halifax I hear. She weighs 12 kilograms (27 pounds) and they says she's 140 years old. They call her Clarissa; I don't know why. Lobsters ought to be between 0.5 and 2 kilograms (1–4 pounds) for good eating.

Nova Scotia is well-known for boat building and for its fishing, of course, but it's also a place where there's steel, coal, wood products and apples. Halifax is our capital city with a population of about 100,000. The population of the whole province does not even total 1,000,000.

The land area of Nova Scotia is about 5 million hectares (20,000 square miles). People tell me that it looks a lot like Scotland with its rolling hills and long, rocky coastline. I guess that's why it's called Nova Scotia or 'New Scotland'. It is the most easterly point of Canada's mainland – the first stop for ships from Europe. The earliest settlers were immigrants from Scotland and when you first arrive in Nova Scotia you may be greeted in Gaelic with: 'Ciad mile failte'. Translated into English, this means 'A hundred thousand welcomes'.

'In Ontario we have 400,000 lakes'

Art Elmhirst is in his early seventies. He has been flying for nearly 50 years. He began his flying career with a tiny single-engine biplane called a Gypsy Moth. This was back when the folk hero of young Canadians, the bush pilot, was in his heyday. It was an era of romance and risk and high adventure, and it's not over yet.

I would describe a bush pilot as the fellow who flies a light aircraft into remote parts of the country to provide communications, delivery and rescue services to areas where there is no other practical link with the outside world. I am talking about the millions of square kilometres of bush (or forest) and mountains in the northern part of our central and western provinces and up to the Arctic Circle and beyond. In summer the bush pilot's aircraft is equipped with floats; in winter the same aircraft is fitted with skis.

The early bush planes included the Fairchild, the Gypsy Moth and the Fox Moth. Bush aircraft have become far more sophisticated over the years, but they are still pretty small machines so that they can get in and out of small places. Today there are regular airlines servicing the larger communities in the north like Whitehorse, Yellowknife, Fort Churchill and Frobisher Bay, but the remote districts still depend on the bush pilot for supply and rescue services. I fly people into the bush, to remote lakes that are almost impossible to reach except by air, but I am taking them in for holidays. Some of the lakes have never been fished. This is not too difficult to understand when you consider that in Ontario alone we have 400,000 lakes. I will fly a party in to a remote lake for a day of fishing or for an overnight stay and come back and pick them up at the end of that time. Fly-in holidays, as we call them, are quite common in the Canadian wilderness. Visitors can spend as much as a week or two on an isolated lake fishing and canoeing. We also fly visitors on quick sightseeing trips over our own lake or on longer trips farther north.

In Canada there is a vast geological formation called the Precambrian or Canadian Shield which forms a gigantic horseshoe with Hudson Bay in the centre. This formation extends from north-eastern Quebec Province down into northern Ontario, and up again into north-western Canada. It is a region of rock and lakes and trees, full of gold, silver, copper, nickel,

Art takes his passengers on fishing or camping holidays to Canada's isolated lakes.

zinc and many other valuable metals. There is very little population. The fly-in lakes we take visitors to are at the southern edge of the Shield, about 150 kilometres (95 miles) north of here. I take them there in either a two-passenger or a four-passenger float plane and we land right on the surface of the lake.

Apparently float planes are not too common in Europe. I suppose there aren't so many lakes there. Because of this we get pilots here from West Germany, Britain, the Republic of Ireland and some other countries who want to learn to fly a float plane. Officially it's called a seaplane, even though they are used far from the sea. We train the pilots with about five hours in the aircraft and two on the ground and they leave here with a float endorsement to their pilot's licence that is recognized anywhere in the world. We also have a small grass landing strip for use when aircraft have wheels rather than floats. I've been flying for nearly fifty years now and my ambition is to go on doing so for as long as I can.

Art checks the fuel in his float plane before taking off from his base, Lake Rice.

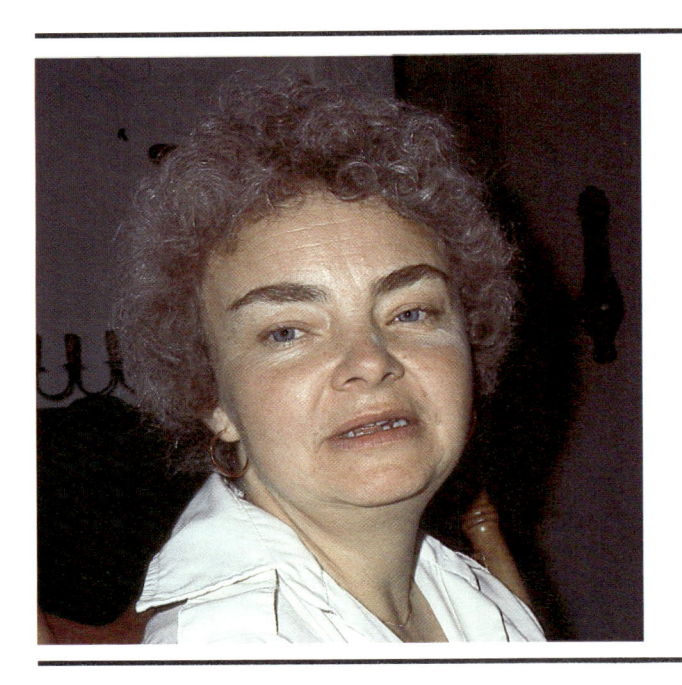

'Canada was developed because of hats'

Sharon Armstrong is in charge of the staff, mostly university students, who play the rôles of early French settlers in Ste. Marie Among the Hurons, the reconstructed site of the first European settlement in Ontario.

Ste. Marie Among the Hurons presents an exciting picture of Canada's early history. Three hundred and fifty years ago it was the centre of the French Jesuit Christian mission to the native Huron people. As a result of the Huron-Iroquois Indian wars Ste. Marie was abandoned and burned by the missionaries.

After decades of archaeological and historical research twenty-two buildings were reconstructed on the original foundations. Today, the everyday life of that iso-

Sharon watches as Marie Brunelle, who is Algonquin Indian and French, shucks corn into the open-fire cooking pot.

The reconstructed seventeenth-century French community of Ste. Marie Among the Hurons.

lated community of the early 1600s is expertly brought to life as a living monument to those early pioneering days so that visitors — particularly school children — can touch the cutlery and work with the blacksmith or the baker and can sense history. My job here is interpreter. That means someone who interprets the parksite to visitors, not someone who translates from one language to another.

The Jesuits came to Canada to convert the natives to Christianity. They had become acquainted with the Huron people in Quebec. The Huron were farmers, which meant that they stayed for long periods of time in one place and were thus accessible to the missionaries. Other tribes, such as the Iroquois, were essentially hunters and led a nomadic existence. So the priests chose to come to the prime location of the Huron, the Georgian Bay area of what is now Ontario. Back in the 1600s the British hadn't come this far as they were occupied with the fur trade along the Atlantic seaboard and in what is now New York State, south of Lake Ontario. This area was part of New France; it wasn't yet known as Canada.

The Jesuits and their helpers came by canoe — 1,280 kilometres (800 miles) from Quebec along the St. Lawrence, Ottawa and Mattawa Rivers, and down Georgian Bay to where the town of Midland now stands. They carried cattle and seed, and all their tools and strips of iron for making nails in these canoes. When they came to rapids or when they ran out of lake, they carried the canoes and all the cargo on their backs through the bush and overland to the next water. They called this a portage. (There are still streets in Canadian cities named Portage after those back-breaking treks overland by the early explorers and settlers.)

The Jesuits weren't directly involved in the fur trade, although the French explorers, like the British of that time, most certainly were. It seems a bit odd today to look back and realize that Canada was developed 350 years ago because of hats: fur hats. I'm not talking about the kind of hats frontiersmen wear, with the racoon tail hanging down the back. I'm talking about a refined, tailored, floppy-brimmed, high-crowned hat made from the fine inner fur of the beaver and worn by European high society. For this men died; wars were fought between France and Britain to establish territorial rights over the areas where the fur trading was being carried out. The Huron nation was all but wiped out as a result of this struggle, by the diseases brought by the Europeans from which the Huron had no immunity, and the actual warfare over the fur trade between Huron and Iroquois. The white man's gift was a sorry one indeed to the North American Indian.

'Toronto is the financial centre of Canada'

Monica Lacock lives in Toronto, Canada's largest English-speaking city. She is a hostess at Toronto's famous CN Tower, the tallest free-standing structure in the world. She is 20 years old and a student in tourism at a college north of the city.

When my parents came to Toronto, before I was born, it was not a very exciting place. People used to go to Montreal for a good time or across the border to one of the American cities. This part of Canada was known as WASP country. WASP meant White Anglo-Saxon Protestant, which described the majority of the population at that time. Then people began to come here from many foreign lands. They brought their customs and their cooking with them and Toronto and southern Ontario became a lot more interesting. Now the Americans come here for a good time.

Today Toronto has a population of about 2,500,000. This includes 400,000 Italians, 200,000 Germans, thousands of Greeks, Portuguese, Japanese, Chinese, East Indians, Ukrainians, Poles, Caribbeans, and Americans. My father came from Yugoslavia; my mother from West Germany.

The city is full of public parks and trees line the streets so that when I look down on it from the CN Tower it looks like a city

The CN Tower is struck by lightning about 200 times each year.

growing out of a forest. Even though it is the financial centre of Canada, millions of visitors come here every year.

I'm called a CN Tower hostess. Every day I do five or six different jobs, rotating every hour. All of them involve working with the public. I'm paid about $4 an hour and I work an eight hour day.

The CN Tower stands 553 metres (1,815 feet) high. Despite its huge success as a tourist attraction its main purpose is to provide a platform for transmitting equipment for Toronto's TV and FM radio stations. Today there are seven FM transmitters and six TV transmitters on the CN Tower. By increasing the height of their transmitters in this way the broadcasters can greatly increase the distance over which their signals can be received, particularly in the highly built-up areas. The greatest concentration of population in all Canada is along the north shore of Lake Ontario, around the western tip, where there is much heavy industry, and down to the Niagara Peninsula. The TV and FM signals from the tower also penetrate the United States on the south side of Lake Ontario.

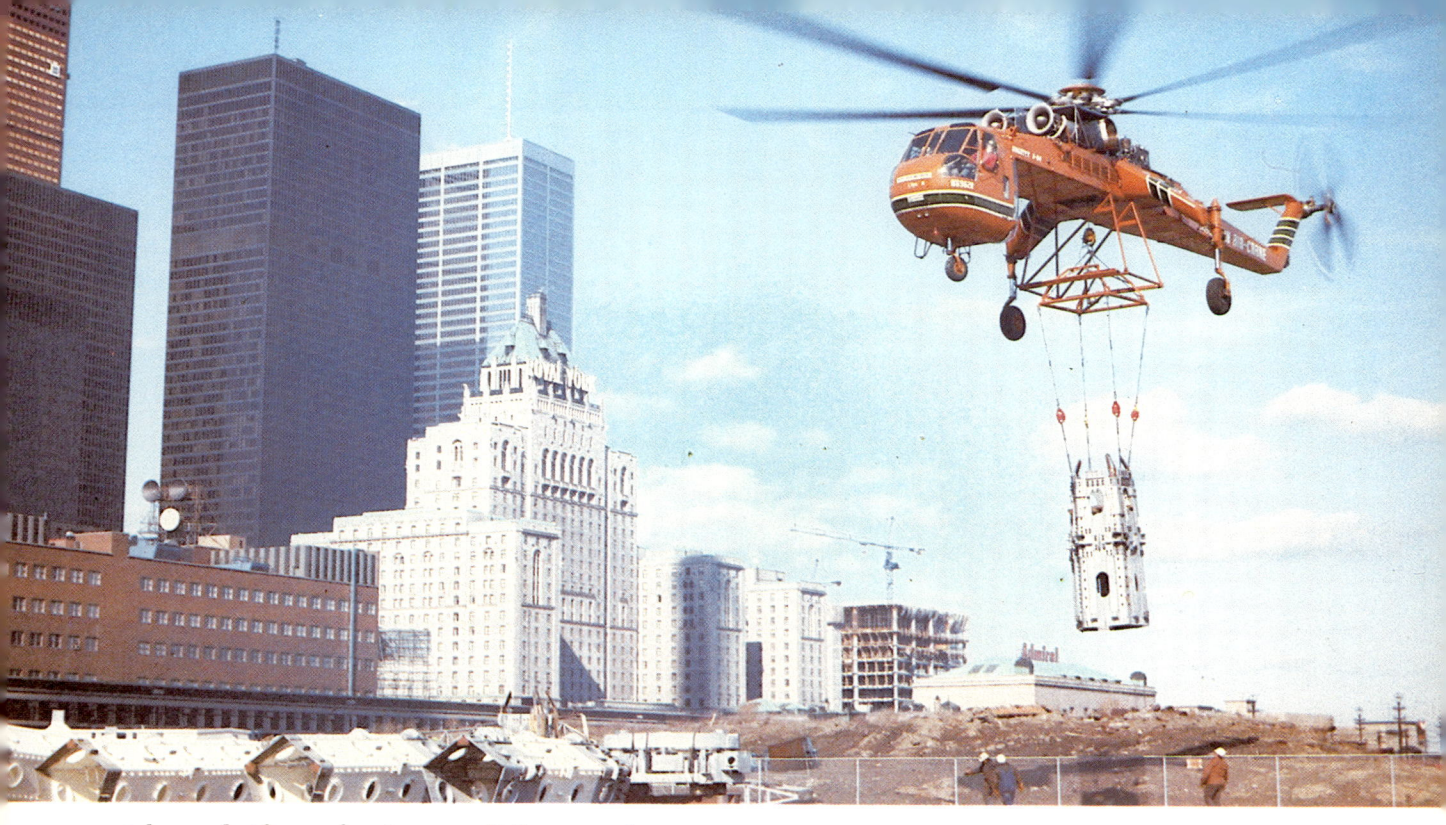

This is just a summer job for me. I've been here about three months. I am going to school right now, to a community college where I am studying tourism. My first year was all business. In my second year I studied many aspects of transportation, learning about different airlines, hotel

During the construction of the CN Tower a powerful sky-crane helicopter was used to move the top sections into position.

management, and personal selling. We also took French. I can already speak German because of my mother, but in Canada you need to know French too as about a quarter of the population speaks French as a first language.

With the money I earn at my summer jobs I pay my own way through college. Most of my friends earn their own way through school. It's quite usual in Canada. For fun I like to travel. I've been to our Pacific coast and the Rocky Mountains, and I love to visit Quebec Province.

Probably the thing I like most about living in Canada is the great geographical variety we have – huge mountains, great plains, hundreds of thousands of lakes, hot summers and snow-filled winters, and thousands of kilometres of rugged, beautiful coastline.

27

'Some moose weigh as much as 800 kilograms'

Ron Tozer is a native Canadian. He lives just outside Algonquin Park, which is a 777,000-hectare (3,000-square-mile) nature reserve in Ontario where he works as a park naturalist. He is married and has a son and a daughter, aged 7 and 10, who are also interested in the Canadian outdoors.

This country still abounds with wild animals. There are moose, deer, beaver, antelope, bears, big cats, killer whales, mountain sheep, buffalo, lynx, otter, eagles, and hawks. The great brown bears of north-west Canada and Alaska are the largest living land carnivores. They grow up to 680 kilograms (1,500 pounds).

My job here at Algonquin Park is to introduce park visitors to the human and natural history of this area to increase their enjoyment and understanding of their own country. There are more than 130

The reds, golds and yellows of the maples in Algonquin Park in autumn.

parks in this province alone and many more across the country.

Animals indigenous to this area are deer, moose, black bear, beaver, lynx and bobcat, wolves, fox, otter, squirrel, chipmunk, skunk, stoat and marten. The timber wolf is well known and people come from all over to hear him baying at the moon, or whatever it is he bays at. We sometimes take visitors to places where the wolves have been heard and do wolf calls. The wolves often answer.

You can often see moose in the spring out on the verge of the highway. We have about a thousand moose at the park. Some weigh as much as 800 kilograms (1,760 pounds). Other than the moose, which is found from the Atlantic Ocean to the Pacific, the main large wild animals are found in the west. The famous grizzly bear lives in the mountains of Canada's west coast. He is the fiercest and strongest of the wild bears. He is called grizzly because of the yellow-tipped long hairs which are backed by black roots so that the bear has a grey appearance. His nickname is 'Silvertip'. He eats calves, ponies, deer and sometimes humans. He is a favourite target for big game hunters.

The polar bear lives in the Arctic. He is pure white and lives mostly in the water. He eats fish, seals, wolves and birds if he can catch them. The polar bear is a fierce fighter and sometimes attacks humans, but his cousin the black bear is pretty peaceful. He is found in the wooded regions all across Canada. He is black with a brown snout. Sometimes he is reddish-brown and is called a cinnamon bear. Black bears are omnivorous. They eat berries, fish, nuts, insects, frogs, snakes, roots and honey. (They aren't bothered at all by bee stings.) Sometimes, if foraging is difficult, they will eat small pigs and sheep.

Canada has abundant wildlife including large bears like this one.

The black bear hibernates for six months of the year. It is during this time that the young are born.

The only serious problem with black bears is people. The bear doesn't have good eyesight. He isn't in the habit of watching where he is going. He is so strong that all the other animals watch out for him. So if he runs across another animal in the woods (you) he assumes you are either another bear or something to eat.

There are lions in Canada too – mountain lions. These are officially known as members of the puma family who have cousins in Africa. We call them cougars.

One of the major crises facing naturalists and conservationists in Canada is acid rain. None of our 2,456 lakes in Algonquin is clinically dead yet, but we are only 320 kilometres (200 miles) from industrial Ontario and the United States. This area is extremely vulnerable. We must get together with our own industrialists and the Americans and work out a solution. There's no mystery. We know exactly how to take care of this problem of pollution. I think there is reason for hope. I think we can do it.

'I drive 160 kilometres a day to work'

Pat Cummins is 34 and employed in the oil business in Alberta. He is a geologist with Pan Canadian Petroleum. His province produces approximately 1,000,000 barrels of oil each day and, as a result, Canada is very nearly self-sufficient in oil.

My job is to explore for oil and gas and this is done by geologically mapping the sub-surface rock formations. Based on the resulting maps we drill wells into the ground in an attempt to find either an oil or a gas pool. Oil is found in what are known as sedimentary rocks. These are rocks which have tiny holes or pores in them and they occur in areas which were once covered by water.

Alberta is in western Canada, combining the flatlands of the prairies in its eastern extremities, with the Rocky Mountains where it borders British Columbia in the west. It has a population of 2,250,000. This province is known for its cowboys and cattle ranches, which run about 900,000 head of beef cattle, and for its highly productive oil wells. Alberta produces approximately 1,000,000 barrels of oil a day and it ships oil and natural gas across Canada.

The first indication of natural gas in Alberta was a fluke. About a century ago when the construction of the Canadian

Much of Pat's time as a geologist is spent in the laboratory.

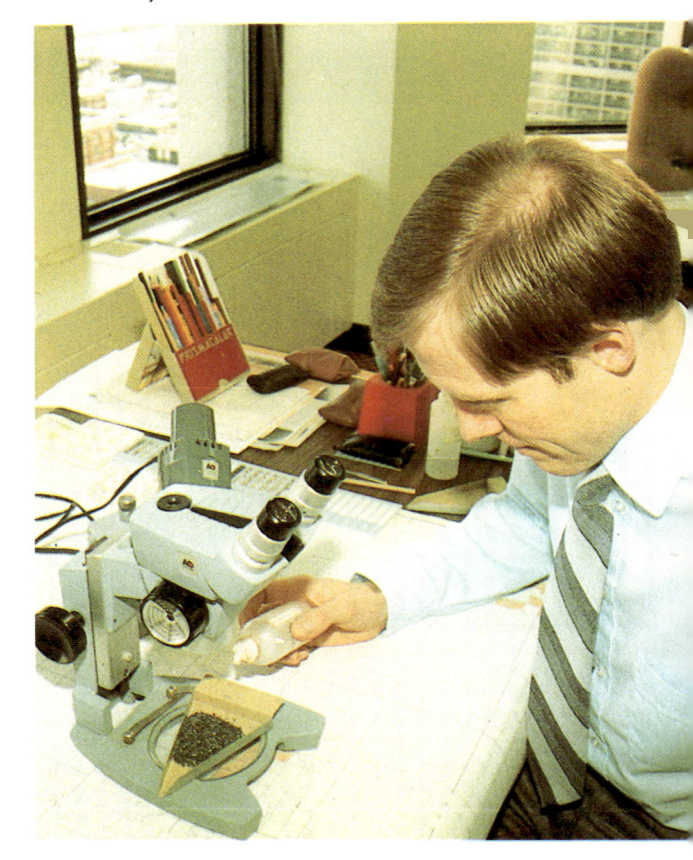

An oil production pump on the flat prairies of Alberta where Pat works.

Pacific Railway had progressed across the prairies and was heading into the mountains, a strange thing happened in the Alberta flatlands. Despite the fact that Canada has the world's greatest supply of fresh water, supplies on the great plains were scarce and the railway needed lots of fresh water to supply the steam locomotives used at that time. So the railroaders were constantly drilling for water close to the track. In December 1883, a crew was drilling for water near what is now Medicine Hat, and instead of hitting a pocket of water they hit natural gas. The gas rushed up the tube and caught fire when it reached the surface. The fire destroyed the wooden rig and the surrounding work buildings and some of the crew were injured. However, once they got over their shock, the rail crews began to look for ways of harnessing the natural gas. They used it to power drilling equipment and for heating.

Since then organizations such as my company, Pan Canadian Petroleum Limited, have been locating, processing, and delivering natural gas all across Canada. It was known that oil was present in Alberta at least fifty years ago, but I don't think it sparked much exploration, mainly because economically speaking it was very hard to get at. Then, in 1947, there was a rather spectacular find at a place called Leduc, near the Alberta capital of Edmonton. The Leduc find demonstrated that there were enormous oil fields in the province and oil company exploration accelerated from that time. Today we produce and refine oil in huge quantities and sell it across Canada and to the United States. Now Canada is very nearly self-sufficient in petroleum products.

I live on a small farm, or ranch, about 80 kilometres (50 miles) north west of Calgary. This means I drive a round trip of 160 kilometres (100 miles) every day to come to work. Where we live is what we call foothill country, where it is rolling terrain leading up to the Rocky Mountains. You can always see the Rockies on the western horizon with their snow-capped peaks jutting up into the sky. I was born, brought up, educated and am now employed in this part of Canada.

'I get an allowance of $1 a week'

Jacquelyn Fraser is 11. She lives on one of Canada's 91,000 dairy farms where 2,500,000 cows each produce about 4,500 litres (1,000 gallons) of milk and cream each year. Hers is a family farm that specializes in Holsteins.

I've lived all my life on the farm in a place in southern Ontario called Brampton. My responsibilities on the farm, include feeding the cows when the hired men have their days off, and helping with the milking by washing the udders and putting dip on after they are milked. I also take care of the calves, usually about fifteen or sixteen of them. Around the house I am responsible for cutting the lawn. For this we use the kind of lawn mower that you sit on and drive. It takes about 1½ hours. I keep my own room tidy and help with the dishes. I get an allowance of $1 a week and I can do whatever I like with it.

All our cattle are milk cattle. They are called Holsteins. Those are the black and white ones, although sometimes one comes along that is red and white. We don't have any beef cattle. We run about 150 head of Holsteins. Our barns are painted black and white to go with the cows. Our best cow is called Spring Farm Citation Rosetta. She is a champion cow and we use her for breeding purposes. In the ten years of her breeding life so far she has had twenty-four heifers. Rosetta's heifers sell for anywhere between $16,000 and $250,000. I guess that's why she's worth $1,000,000. We sell her calves to places like Italy and the United States.

Jacquelyn with her treasured dairy cow – Spring Farm Citation Rosetta.

I've been in the Girl Guides about three years and I have earned twenty-two badges. You earn a badge for things like milking a cow, camping, pet keeping, gardening, team sport, and cooking (I helped my mum make a meal). I'm now working on my seamstress badge.

I plan to go to the University of Guelph, which is quite near here, so that I can be a veterinarian when I grow up. I like animals. I chose Guelph because my dad went there. To go to university you have to have Grade 13 and by that time I'll be 17 or 18 years old. Right now I go to a school down the road. Kids from all over the area go there in an orange school bus.

The school year runs from the first week in September until the end of June. The school day starts at 8.30 in the morning and ends at 2.45 in the afternoon. For holidays we have two weeks in summer, ten or twelve days at Christmas and what we call mid-winter break – one week in March.

Jacquelyn using a drill at school. One of her favourite subjects is industrial arts.

I like school. My favourite subjects are art, French, English composition and industrial arts, which we call 'shops'. In shops we build things out of wood and use saws and drills and planes. It used to be that only boys took shops, but now both girls and boys take it. I suppose I do about one hour's homework a night right now, but there will be more when I get into the higher grades.

I like to swim and I'm learning to play the piano. I used to take figure skating. We have a swimming pool that's about 12 metres (40 feet) long and once I did fifty lengths. I also like to cycle. But what I like to do best is play baseball. I'm on the local team and I play left field. I also like to curl. In our team we don't use the full-sized curling rocks because they weigh twenty kilograms (forty-four pounds). We use what are called jam-tin rocks. That's a can full of cement that has had a handle stuck in it. It weighs about seven kilograms (fifteen pounds). We aim our jam-tin rocks at a sort of target that is marked on the ice at each end of the rink.

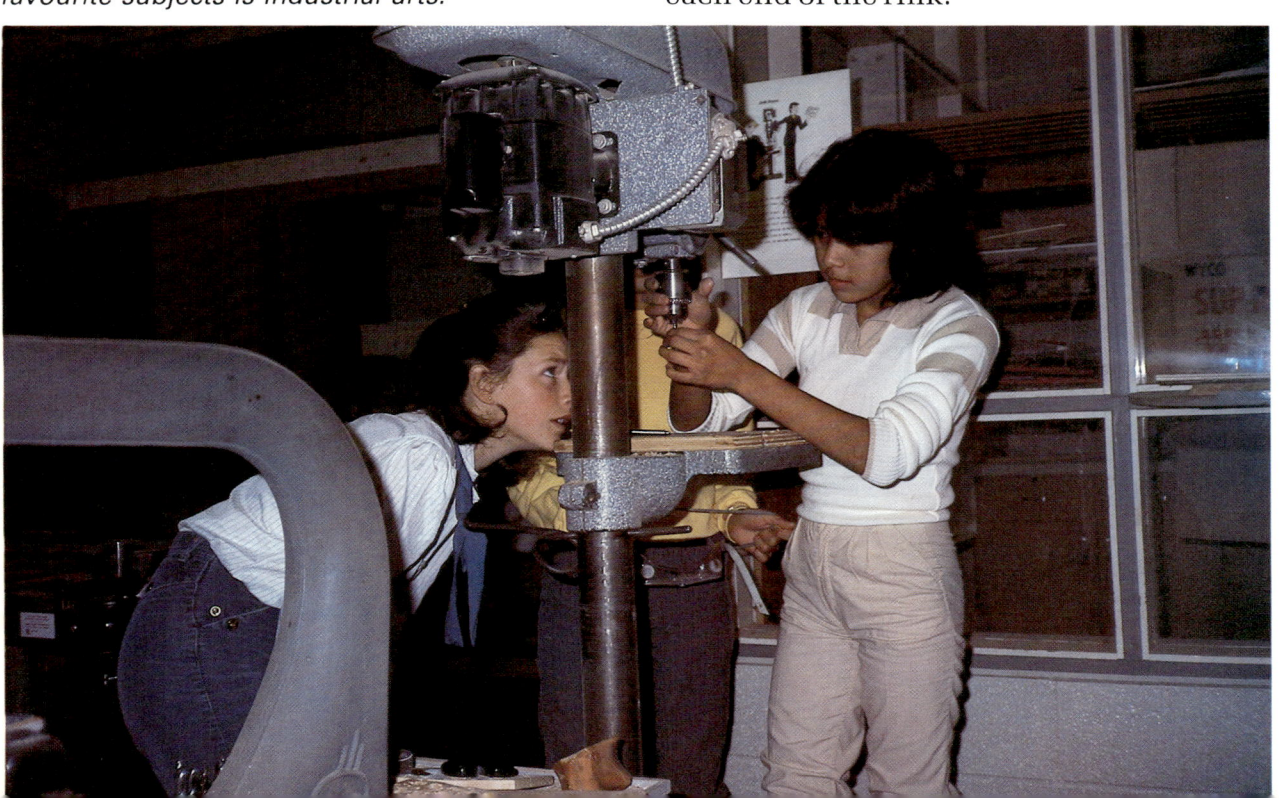

'The oldest colony and the youngest province'

John Crosbie is a federal politician, from Newfoundland. The province of Newfoundland comprises an island off the east coast of Canada and a large section of the mainland, called Labrador. It is rich in oil and natural gas.

I am a federal member of parliament in Ottawa, representing the Newfoundland riding of St. John's West. An MP's function is to represent his political party and his constituency at the federal level, to gain for them whatever aid and support he can.

The Canadian Houses of Parliament in Ottawa where John is an MP.

Newfoundland is Canada's tenth province. Its area is about 41.5 million hectares (160,000 square miles) with a population of about 600,000.

The island was settled mainly for the fishing, and any settlement inland has been the result of the growth of specific industries like hydro-electric development, mining, pulp and paper. We are rich in oil and natural gas reserves but there is very little agriculture. The soil is thin. During the ice age the glacial movement scraped most of the topsoil off the island and deposited it in the sea so that the farming is done mainly in the ocean — in the Grand Banks which is the world's richest fishing area. The main occupation of the people of my province is fishing and many hundreds of small settlements exist along the abundant coastline.

Sir Humphrey Gilbert took possession of Newfoundland in 1583 on behalf of the queen of England, Elizabeth I. It is said that this was the foundation for the creation of the British Empire. In the early days

Newfoundland had dominion status just as Canada, Australia and New Zealand had in later years. But in 1933 the Newfoundland government ran into hard times and had to ask Britain for financial assistance to meet interest payments on its national debt. Britain agreed to assist Newfoundland only if we surrendered our responsible government. So we reverted to a government of three English commissioners and three Newfoundland commissioners appointed by the Colonial Office in Britain. They ran Newfoundland until 1949. Then we became a province of Canada So Newfoundland is Britain's oldest colony and Canada's youngest province.

In Ottawa the House of Commons, to which I belong, sits about nine months of the year. There are 282 seats. Our Senate, or upper house, has 104 seats. It does a lot of good work in committee, but only about half the members of the Senate give you an honest day's work and the rest are ready for retirement. I like politics. You either have it in your blood or you don't; it's like a disease.

Canada is not in particularly good shape economically right now, but when you look around the world and see what the options are you have to accept that in Canada the prospects are still better than in most countries.

The shores of John Crosbie's home province – Newfoundland – are dotted with small communities like this one.

'Regina used to be called Pile-of-Bones'

Dave Ridgeway is 25 and a place kicker for the Saskatchewan Roughriders football team. He was born in England but is now a Canadian citizen. He lives in Regina, the capital of the province of Saskatchewan which is in the middle of the vast Canadian prairies.

I'm the second smallest guy on my team. I weigh 86 kilograms (190 pounds) and I stand 1.85 metres (6 feet 1 inch) tall. In my business that's small. On the field I have to watch out for the big guys. They come as big as 2 metres (6 feet 7 inches) tall and 127 kilograms (280 pounds).

During a Canadian football match only twelve men are allowed on the field at any one time for each team. You score points by moving the ball across the opposing team's goal line at the end of the field. You can carry it across, which gives you what's called a touchdown. Or you can kick it through the upright goal-posts.

I'm a place kicker on the Saskatchewan Roughriders football team. I am number 36. A place kicker kicks field goals when his team can't get into the opposition's end zone. And I kick extra points when my team scores a touchdown. During an entire football game, which lasts at least a couple

Dave does some practice kicking before the start of a big match.

36

Kick-off in the match between the Roughriders and the Toronto Argonauts.

of hours, I may spend only four or five minutes on the field.

The ball is elliptical and is made of pigskin. You can carry, throw or kick the ball down the field. The opposing team tries to prevent you from doing this by getting in the way of the ball if you are kicking, or by getting in the way of you if you are carrying it. They are allowed to tackle only the man who is carrying the ball. All the while your team is trying to get down to the other team's goal line, that team is trying to take the ball away from your team and get it across your goal line. You are allowed a series of attempts, called 'downs', to move the ball toward the opposition's goal line. You must move the ball at least ten yards (nine metres) in three downs. If you don't succeed in advancing ten yards you forfeit the ball to the other team and they try to move it towards your goal line.

The Roughriders are based in the city of Regina in the middle of the Canadian prairies. The original name of this city was Pile-of-Bones. In the language of the plains Indians this was 'Wascana'. Apparently when the prairies were first being settled there used to be great buffalo hunts. Thousands and thousands of buffalo would be slaughtered for their meat and hides, and the bones would be hauled to the site of what is now Regina where there was a railroad. I saw a photograph of it and I could hardly believe it. Buffalo bones were piled six metres (twenty feet) high by the railway tracks waiting to be shipped east to be used in the production of bone china. So the little village at that point on the railroad was called Pile-of-Bones. Later it was renamed Regina. I think I like Regina better.

37

'Mining is big business in Canada'

Robin Rose is 37 and a driller in one of Canada's 300 operating mines. He works more than a kilometre underground in Sudbury, Ontario, helping to extract nickel and copper from the depths of the earth.

Prince Edward Island is my home. It's sometimes called 'Spud Island' because potatoes are the main agricultural crop there. There are no mines on the island, though. I wanted to be a miner and that's why I came here to Sudbury in 1970.

I am a driller in the Stobie mine. Here we try to extract copper and nickel. The mine belongs to INCO, which stands for the International Nickel Company. When I'm working below, I use a hand-held pneumatic drill to bore holes in the rock face for blasting. Then we pack the holes with explosive and stand clear.

The exact origin of the rock structure in the Sudbury region is not known. But a popular theory is that at one time, hundreds of millions of years ago, a tremendous meteor came crashing into this area from space making a crater about 24 by 64 kilometres (15 by 40 miles). The impact caused a crack in the ancient rock crust allowing molten rock from the earth's core to ooze into the new formation.

The rich nickel and copper deposits were actually found here by accident. A hundred years ago, when railroad crews were working in this region to build the trans-Canada railway, their blasting unearthed rock which contained deposits of nickel, copper and some other minerals. This started a real land rush, as prospectors swarmed in and began to dig.

Today mining is big business in Canada. There are more than 300 operating mines

Robin makes the long journey to the face, over a kilometre below ground level.

across the country and the various companies that own them employ seven per cent of all working Canadians. From these mines about sixty different commodities are extracted including nickel, copper, gold, silver, platinum, coal and iron.

Underground, I work with a partner. We both do the same job, working side by side. As a driller I am paid $10.92 an hour. I am trying at present to perfect my skills on the 'scoop', which is a power shovel, and a 'jumbo', which is a pneumatic drill system mounted on a big machine. When I have learned how to work these machines I can become a trackless miner. A trackless miner gets paid $11.39 an hour. In mining you can try for any job that comes along.

The INCO works at Sudbury. The 'superstack' chimney is 380 metres (1,250 feet) high.

The man with the most seniority gets the job. Some men have been working in the mines for forty years, so they always get first choice.

In my spare time I like to cross-country ski. I am married and have three children, a girl and two boys. We all ski together although the little guy (Marty is just 5) only started last winter so he isn't very good yet. Once I took part in a cross-country ski marathon from Lachute, in Quebec, to Ottawa. That was about 160 kilometres (100 miles) and provided a real contrast to my usual work underground.

'Mounties are like the feathers on a bird'

Royal Canadian Mounted Police Constable Ian MacDonald comes from Ottawa. He is 32 and a member of the Yukon detachment of Canada's federal police force, based in Whitehorse. Ian often has to work in temperatures of minus 50°C.

There are three levels of law enforcement in Canada. At the federal level there is the Royal Canadian Mounted Police (RCMP). There are provincial police in two of our ten provinces. And, of course, there is a law enforcement function at the municipal level, the city or town police. The RCMP, however, is in a unique position because it functions at all three levels. In the eight provinces and two territories where there is no provincial or territorial police force, the Mounties handle the work. In many small communities which don't have their own local police, again the Mounties are asked to handle law enforcement. Fortunately, all three levels work successfully with each other.

In the Yukon Division of the RCMP we have 126 members. Of these 116 are white including nine women, nine are Indian, one is Eskimo and there is also one dog. If you should apply the 126 members to the

The Mounties wear their familiar red uniforms only on ceremonial occasions.

Ian in his working uniform, looks across the Yukon River at the old paddle steamer Klondike.

area of Yukon Territory, which is 536,326 square kilometres (207,076 square miles) that works out (not counting the dog) to 4,256 square kilometres (1,643 square miles) for each Mountie.

Throughout their history neither the Mounties nor their predecessors the North-West Mounted Police (NWMP), ever fought the Indians. Our function did not parallel that of the US Cavalry. One of the senior plains Indian chiefs said of the Mounties: 'They are like the feathers of a bird. The feathers protect the bird from the cold.' The NWMP and latterly the RCMP protected the Indian people. One of our biggest concerns in early days was the whisky trader who created havoc among our native people.

The Yukon is still gold mining country, and the fur trade is extremely active. One Indian here grosses $40,000 every winter from his trapline alone. He goes after gold in the summer. We are also busy with tourists. This summer 393,000 tourists passed through here. It was one of our best years, bringing in $50,000,000. Visitors love to canoe on the Yukon River. We keep regular patrols on the river to be sure they don't get into trouble. The water is bitterly cold winter and summer.

We wear knee-length Arctic parkas in winter. These have a big hood framed in wolverine fur. This fur doesn't freeze because the hairs are hollow. We wear muskrat fur hats with ear flaps, thick-soled boots or mukluks, heavy whipcord pants, heavily lined leather gloves, and long underwear. Even then we have to keep moving to stay warm. For transportation we use patrol cars, aircraft, both fixed wing and helicopters, boats of all kinds, and snow machines. I am not a pilot, but I'm checked out on cars and motorcycles. The cold can be so deep and penetrating that even metal can shatter under stress. It is important, if you are travelling by car through this area, that you take warm blankets, candy bars for emergency nourishment, and candles to heat the inside of your vehicle if you're stranded for any length of time. A candle will provide enough heat to keep you going.

Despite all the talk about the harsh climate, the summers in the Yukon are very pleasant. The sun shines for twenty hours each day. In between the mountains, like Mount Logan which rises to 6,050 metres (19,850 feet), there is fertile soil in the flatlands and crops like grain and vegetables grow in an astonishingly short time. Big paddlewheel steamers used to ply the rivers during the summer.

'You gotta heal well and heal quick'

Ron Hartill is a logger on Vancouver Island, which is part of Canada's most westerly province, British Columbia. He earns about $200 for a 6½-hour day. Ron is 47, and seven-times world champion lumberjack in international competitions.

The Douglas firs can grow up to 90 metres (300 feet) high. The red cedar might have a diameter of 6 metres (20 feet) and some of the big ones are estimated to be 1,000 years old. Forestry is British Columbia's first industry and this province's standing timber equals approximately one-quarter of the North American inventory.

There are other industries in British Columbia, such as mining, tourism, agriculture, and fishing, but forestry is number one. Almost all the forest land is owned or administered by the provincial government. The principal of a sustained yield applies here. We keep planting new trees so that the forests do not get depleted.

Logging can be dangerous work, and in the woods probably the most dangerous job of all is the faller's. I am a faller and my job is to cut down the trees and then buck (or cut) them into the required length for the mills — about 13 metres (44 feet). The tree you're cutting down isn't the risk. The danger comes from what can shake loose as you start to cut into a tree. About 60 metres (200 feet) above your head there might be a limb caught in the branches that had been knocked loose by a storm. Just the vibration of your chain-saw might loosen the limb and send it crashing down. Fallers have been wiped out this way. Worse than that is a dead tree that is broken apart by the vibration of the saw and comes down on top of you. I've been injured lots of times. In this work you gotta heal well and heal quick.

The first into the woods are the grade crews who hack out roads so you can get the trees out. Then come the fallers. After the fallers the rigging crew moves in and puts up a tower and pulley system to pull the logs out by line to the spur roads where they are loaded on to trucks. Then the truck crews haul them to the 'dryland sort' where they are sorted according to species, bundled, and dumped into the water to go by boom down to the mill. A boom is a lot of logs held together like a big wooden island and then manoeuvred through the water to the mill. In the mill, here at Lake Cowichan, they produce planks or timber of different sizes and there is a veneer plant where they make plywood. These products are all trucked to the railhead or one of the ocean ports.

I've taken part in a lot of what we call loggers' sports. I have been seven times the world champion lumberjack through international loggers' sport competitions.

Once cut, the logs are then floated in a boom to the sawmill.

Much tree-felling in Canada is now done by machine.

The events include the underhand chop and the vertical chop with an axe; the springboard chop where you stand on a board inserted into the trunk of a tree that is difficult to reach from the ground; sawing with a two-metre (seven-foot) crosscut saw; axe throwing; speed-climbing up a tree; and a number of chain-saw events. I enjoy them all. Particularly the ones I win.

'The Rockies are the backbone of North America'

Banff Springs Hotel perches high in the Rocky Mountains and is one of Canada's most famous resort hotels. It has 579 rooms and caters to an international clientele. Robert MacLean is a sous chef. He likes to cook, ski and fish. He is 32.

I started cooking when I was 14. Today I am a sous chef at Banff Springs Hotel, one of the best known hotels in the Canadian Pacific chain. I am a supervisor in charge of organizing the kitchen here and I oversee the staff, cooking and presenting meals in the hotel.

It takes sixty-five people to run this kitchen, exclusive of the staff that are needed to serve in the dining room. The kitchen opens each morning at five o'clock to handle the early risers. Here we put a menu together for speed. We do have our special dishes, but the people who stay at Banff Springs Hotel are here to explore the Rocky Mountains. They want to be out looking around, and don't have a lot of time for meals. They are conscious of nutrition and they like variety, but their main concern is to get out into the mountains and enjoy the outdoors. The Rockies are the backbone of North America. They form a nearly continuous chain from the Arctic almost to the northern border of Mexico. They are the continental divide. Many major rivers start in the Rockies and, depending on which side of the mountains they lie, they then flow into the Pacific Ocean or the Arctic Ocean. The Saskatchewan, the Mackenzie, the Peace and the Athabaska end up directly or indirectly in the Arctic. The Columbia, the Fraser and the Yukon flow the other way.

The Canadian Rockies are the most spectacular part of the system. They mark the provincial boundary between Alberta

Robert completes a fat sculpture in the dining room at the Banff Springs Hotel.

and British Columbia. Banff is in Alberta.

The superb scenery in the Rocky Mountains makes them a summer and winter playground. As a result many national parks have been set up here such as the Jasper, Banff, Yoho, Kootenay, Revelstoke and Waterton Lakes parks. People come from all over the world to visit the Canadian Rockies and to stay at Banff Springs Hotel.

There isn't one particular dish that is identifiable with the hotel. In summer we keep to light seafoods and fowl. In the winter we serve game food like reindeer, buffalo and rabbit. People enjoy this but there is no great demand. We don't usually prepare special dishes for particular groups of guests. The Japanese, for example, aren't the least bit interested in being fed Japanese food. They are here on holiday and are more interested in eating what we eat.

In my spare time I like to fish and I enjoy skiing, both downhill and cross-country. If you're an avid skier you can find snow to ski on right up to June because of the high mountains. My wife and I also like to go camping in the bush country.

I have a hobby that ties in with my work as a chef. I like to do what is called fat sculpturing. These are the sculptures you often see in the middle of a hotel buffet table. The fat is the same material that's used to make puff pastry. I've done a swan, a koala bear, an explorer, and my next one will be a grizzly bear. They last until someone knocks them over. Then I do another.

The Banff Springs Hotel is set amongst Alberta's Rocky Mountains.

'I have always spoken both languages'

Francine Letellier is 37 and lives in Quebec Province. She is a librarian in the city of Hull, across the Ottawa River from the national capital. The mother tongue of more than 6,000,000 Canadians is French and most of these live in Quebec Province.

I have lived in Quebec City, Montreal, Ottawa and a tiny farming village near Hull called Luskville. In spite of its English name, Hull is essentially a French-speaking community. A small city with all the advantages of a country village. It is a pleasant combination. All around there are nature trails, trees and lakes. Quebec Province is a bit like that with its highly industrialized areas around Montreal — the pulp and paper mills, asbestos mining, copper smelting and aluminium plants — then large remote areas where farmers cling to a culture that goes back to seventeenth-century France.

More than 6,000,000 Canadians use French as their first language, and most of these live in Quebec Province. There are some areas of the province where no English is spoken at all. Quebec is Canada's largest province and Montreal is Canada's largest city. The capital of Quebec Province is Quebec City, located on a high bluff overlooking the St. Lawrence River. An Indian settlement called Stadacona was located on the site when the French explorer Jacques Cartier discovered it. The great river narrows at this point and the name Quebec is the Indian word for strait. It was at this location that the future of Canada was settled in 1759 when the British defeated the French in the Battle of the Plains of Abraham and this country became British.

Old Quebec is surrounded by a heavy wall built by the British in the early

In Quebec Province, all the shops must carry signs in French.

Francine loves to take her children to see the Ice Palace at the Quebec Winter Carnival.

nineteenth century. It is the only walled city in North America. In the streets the modern automobiles contrast with the picturesque, two-wheeled, horse-drawn caleches and, in typical French-Canadian style, the old mixes with the new in both architecture and life styles. I love Quebec City and I go back there whenever I can. I particularly like it at winter carnival time with the ice sculptures – including the beautiful Ice Palace – huge toboggan slide, races across the ice floes in the St. Lawrence River and torchlight skiing.

The working language here in Hull is mainly French. About seventy-five per cent of people speak it, I'd guess. In this library most of our books are in French but the staff are generally bilingual. It bothers a lot of French-Canadians that they have to be the ones who are bilingual rather than the other way around. This doesn't bother me, maybe because some of my ancestors were Scottish. My mother's maiden name was Grant. I have always spoken both languages and I don't remember learning either. As a French-Canadian who speaks English as well, I feel quite comfortable in any part of Canada, but La Belle Province, as Quebec is often known, is my home. Despite the efforts by the federal government to make Canada a completely bilingual country I don't think this is possible. Too much of the country is too far removed from where French is spoken. If you are going to learn a language you have to be surrounded by that language. In North America we are surrounded by English.

In Quebec Province French is the official language. If you run a business in a Quebec community your business signs must, by law, be in French. French-speaking people in this province are afraid that their language will disappear altogether. This could be true.

My children, all boys, are aged 10, 8 and 7. We play football and soccer together. Their first language is French, but they are picking up some English. Children can learn anything. It used to be, when I didn't want them to know what I was talking about, I'd speak English. I can't get away with that any more. They figure it out.

'Canada is an enormous country'

Peter Allchin is 37 and director of airport services for CPAir, one of the two major airlines in Canada. He recognizes that the sheer size of Canada makes air transport the most efficient means of travelling across the country.

My father was an RAF flier in England during World War II and spent time in Canada training Commonwealth air crews. He is now a school teacher. After the war he brought my mother back to Canada to live. They left me to finish school in Blackpool and then in 1963 when I was 17, I was presented with a steamship ticket and a train ticket to join my parents in Alberta. I could hardly believe, when I got here, that it took five days and five nights to cross Canada by train.

Canada is an enormous country. It has

A CPAir Boeing 747 waits on the runway prior to take-off.

an area of nearly 10 million square kilometres (nearly 4 million square miles). From Vancouver on the west coast to Halifax on the east it is over about 6,200 kilometres (nearly 3,879 miles). Yet its population is only about 24 million. People are widely scattered around, so air transport is very important. There is a publicly-owned airline called Air Canada, and the other major airline is CPAir. We are based in Vancouver and our world-wide and domestic route pattern is 101,792 kilometres (63,620 miles). We fly to five continents and to all major cities in Canada and to the far north.

Canadian Pacific first showed an interest in aviation in 1919 when it got a permit from the Canadian Government to own and operate commercial aircraft. Today CPAir is one of the world's major carriers. The man who founded the airline was a bush pilot named Grant McConachie who had been carrying freight and mail and a few passengers in small planes around the remote areas of north-west Canada and up into the snows of the Yukon. He became president of Canadian Pacific Airlines at the age of 38.

My job is to ensure that all passengers of CPAir, flying in and out of Vancouver, get the very best service – ticketing, baggage handling, and anything relating to passenger movement. We think of ourselves as the people's airline and to us service is of the utmost importance. We are a privately-financed organization and we know that if we don't serve the public well they won't come back – we wouldn't be in business the next day. Besides flying people all over Canada, CPAir destinations include Hong Kong, Tokyo, Lima, Santiago, Buenos Aires, Australia, Fiji, Honolulu, Amsterdam, Lisbon, Milan, Rome, Britain and the United States.

We operate forty aircraft including four Jumbo jets (747s) and eight DC 10s. These major aircraft all have names beginning with 'Empress' – *Empress of Australia, Empress of Italy*, and so on. As a matter of fact, the official call sign for any CPAir jet coming in to land is 'Empress'.

There was a day when Canadian Pacific Empress ocean liners were a familiar sight all over the world. They were good, sturdy cruise ships and extremely popular. But today two CPAir 747 jets can carry as many passengers as one of those holiday ocean liners. They travel a good deal faster, too.

I don't think of myself as British, even though I go back to the UK each year. I'm a Canadian. I must admit that people here from time to time do detect a bit of an English accent. They should have heard it twenty years ago!

CPAir fly passengers over some of the most spectacular scenery in the world.

'No one cheered for the Indians'

Gordon Byce is a clergyman, a social counsellor, and part Canadian Indian. His job is to assist handicapped people to lead independent, productive and rewarding lives. His great private interest is to help the Indians.

I was trained as an Anglican clergyman but since 1966 I have been working as a counsellor and I am currently with the Provincial Ministry of Community and Social Services. We help handicapped people with problems that vary from mental retardation to cystic fibrosis. We provide them with counselling, training, books or direct financial support for their day-to-day living.

My mother was a Cree Indian. She was born on an island in James Bay in a place called Moose Factory. The Indians had existed at Moose Factory as a hunting society for hundreds of years but the arrival of the Hudson's Bay Company changed all that. So around the turn of the century her family moved away to Chapleau in northern Ontario. My father was Pennsylvania Dutch. He worked on the railroad which passed through Chapleau. I was born there in 1922.

Growing up as an Indian in a small town I was made to feel that there was something wrong with me; that I was defective.

A Salish Bear totem pole carved by the Cowichan Indians of Canada's west coast.

These Chippewa Indians successfully run a market gardening business on their reserve.

I remember when I was a child and we played cowboys and Indians I never wanted to be Sitting Bull or Crazy Horse; I'd rather be Tom Mix or Roy Rogers. Hollywood movies had something to do with that. No one cheered for the Indians. I went away to theological college and I guess I made it in the white man's society because I never let anyone know at that time that I was Indian. I suppose you could call me a closet Indian. It was fairly late in life before I came to terms with this. It took me a long time to feel the way I feel now about the Indian part of me. My children aren't hung up about it because they've never had any unpleasantness associated with this part of their heritage. They think it's interesting, a romantic sort of thing. They are proud of the Indian part of me.

Officially there are about 300,000 Indians registered in Canada, and about 1,000,000 of mixed blood. Tracts of land called reserves are set aside for the Indian to live on if he chooses. There are 2,200 reserves. A registered Indian is entitled to live on and use the reserve set apart for the band to which he belongs.

But the Indian is caught in a no-man's land when he tries to adjust to the white man's society. He finds he belongs in neither that world nor his own. The Indian does not come from a competitive culture. His culture is essentially co-operative so he has too little of what is necessary to cope with 'western' society. The Indian doesn't fit. He is just too vulnerable.

Some Indians are beginning to work their way into the white man's world becoming lawyers, broadcasters, merchants or whatever. There are Indians who have moved successfully into society, but this is not the general story.

In the English-speaking world we use the word Indian to describe the native people of North America. But this was a name used in error by Christopher Columbus when he reached North America, because he believed he had sailed around the world to India. The Ojibway call themselves 'Anishnabe'. This means 'the people'. That's who we are.

'We do everything together'

Jane McNulty is a teacher, housewife and mother in a little town called Collingwood on Georgian Bay. The entire family skis together and swims together. Jane believes that hers is a typical Canadian family.

We all like to ski. My husband only moved here to Collingwood for the skiing. The town is about 190 kilometres (120 miles) north-west of Toronto on Georgian Bay, which is part of the Great Lakes. In addition to a brisk shipbuilding industry it is an extremely active tourist area.

We live in our own house just outside town and close to Blue Mountain — an ideal place for skiing. Our home is a three-bedroomed bungalow. In Canada about sixty per cent of families own, or are in the process of buying, their own homes. So we are fairly typical, I suppose. We have two children, a boy and a girl, and we do everything together. We ski together, swim, fish and bird-watch together.

I am a teacher by profession. I have a Bachelor of Arts in history and I am currently teaching kindergarten, Grades 1 and 2, and do some work also in Grades 7 and 8. Those are children in the age 13 to 15 range. I teach in what we call a public school. Here in Canada the public school is the publicly financed educational system which all children are required to attend from kindergarten to Grade 8. Until about Grade 5 the children stay in one classroom all day and have the same

Jane's two children, Sarah and Joshua, are expected to help her around the house.

teacher for everything. After that they go on a rotary system. This means they have a 'home room' and a 'home room teacher' but they move from classroom to classroom throughout each day where other teachers teach them specific subjects such as geography or history or English literature.

In this country the public school system is financed by a tax on residences. You can also send your child to what we call a private school, but you pay the tuition fees for this and you must continue to pay your residential taxes. Education in Canada is complicated a bit by the fact that each province has its own system. This was introduced long ago when great distances limited the movement of families back and forth across the country. Today different provinces still have different qualifications for university entry.

Jane, Josh and husband Frank start down Blue Mountain on one of their regular weekend skiing outings.

I was born in Saskatoon, Saskatchewan. The city, Saskatoon, was named by the Indians after a blueberry that grows on the prairies. Saskatchewan is the name of the province and was named after the Saskatchewan River. The Cree Indian word for rapid current is 'kishiska djiwan', and this is where the name 'Saskatchewan' comes from. My family is sixth generation Canadian. I have travelled in Canada as far east as Quebec City and as far west as Saskatoon, and I've been to France, Germany, Holland, England, Italy, Switzerland and Austria. But I haven't been all across Canada yet. I'm going to have to do something about that.

53

'We help make this huge country smaller'

Bob Burt is 42. He is a radio producer for the public broadcasting system, CBC. He believes that radio and TV are essential ingredients to the identity of Canada as a nation. He and his family live in the country.

The fact that Canada exists at all as one country is attributable to the creation of a communications link a century ago that connected the Atlantic and the Pacific Oceans. It was the railroad. Today the need for a workable communications connection across this enormous country is no less real if there is to be any sort of national identity, but now that link is broadcasting – radio and television.

I am a producer with the Canadian Broadcasting Corporation (CBC), the public broadcasting system of Canada. I produce a radio programme called 'Ontario Morning' that is broadcast within a limited network area about 800 kilometres wide and 320 kilometres deep (500 miles by 200 miles). My programme is delivered to a potential audience of about 4,000,000 and is carried by a combination of public and private radio stations.

My show is a mixture of interviews, some music, a little bit of survival information (like road reports, time checks and weather), and a lot of items of particular interest to the many communities which are within range. We are on the air from 6 am to 9 am weekdays.

There are seven time zones in Canada, which means that if you are broadcasting nationally you have to consider this. While your listeners in British Columbia might just be getting out of bed, those in Newfoundland are half-way through their afternoon's work. Fortunately for me, my show serves only one time zone. That makes it a lot easier to programme. The people who listen to 'Ontario Morning' find out what is going on in their own province and also in the rest of the country, and we target mainly for listeners in the smaller communities. We help make this huge country a little bit smaller and more understandable.

The publicly owned CBC is designated by law as the national broadcasting service and it is also Canada's international voice on short-wave. CBC owns and operates more than 900 radio and TV outlets. In addition, there are about 400 privately

The CBC master control unit which channels national radio programmes across seven Canadian time zones.

owned or community owned outlets associated with CBC as radio or TV affiliates. On top of that there are a further 600 privately owned radio and TV stations that operate as independents. It takes a lot of technical equipment to deliver the signals across Canada.

CBC Radio is non-commercial; CBC-TV is a combination of commercial and non-commercial services. The private broadcasting networks are commercial.

I live in the country, about 56 kilometres (35 miles) from the studios. My wife, my three kids and I have 4½ hectares (11 acres) of land complete with a huge swimming pool. It takes five hours to cut the lawn. We have horses and my 12-year-old daughter rides in competitions. We also have our own tennis court. In winter we like downhill skiing. It's a great life and I'm a happy man. If I was any happier I couldn't stand it.

Among CBC's 900 broadcasting outlets are tiny local station centres like this one in Yukon Territory.

'I don't have a lot of spare time'

Teresa Proskurniak is 19, a student and a professional dancer. Her home town is Edmonton, the capital of Alberta. She's danced in three continents but she plans to continue her schooling, possibly to become a lawyer. To her, dancing is just a profitable hobby.

Teresa on the stage with the three-girl and one-man dance group Synergy at the Canadian National Exhibition.

I have been dancing since I was 4. I've danced in Canada, Cyprus, Germany, Israel and I'm expecting to go to Alaska and again to Europe soon. It's lots of fun. It's as if you enjoyed going fishing for a holiday and someone paid you to go fishing.

I was born in Edmonton, the capital of Alberta. Alberta is one of Canada's ten provinces. It is in western Canada, up against the Rocky Mountains. It has an area of about 66 million hectares (255,000 square miles) and my home town, Edmonton, is the largest city. The population of Edmonton is 730,000 which is pretty big for Canada. There are only 2,250,000 people in the entire province. Calgary is the next city with a population of about 600,000. Although I come from the land of the cowboy I can't ride a horse. I tried it when I was 9 and I was a total flop. I haven't been on a horse since.

I dance for money and for fun. I've been trained in tap, ballet, jazz and most of the other styles of dancing. I belong to a group called Synergy. The word means 'combined and correlated force or united action'. That's us. We get most of our work in Edmonton but we've done work overseas and up in the Arctic, at military bases, and this year we had a contract with the Canadian National Exhibition which is in Toronto.

It was my first visit to the Canadian National Exhibition. I hadn't realized how big it was. The famous Calgary Stampede attracts about 1,000,000 visitors each year; the Edmonton Klondike Days bring in about 700,000. The CNE gate has gone as high as 3,500,000. There are exhibitors from Spain, Peru, China, Mexico, the Philippines, the Baltic states, Thailand, Wales, Australia, the Netherlands, the United States – all over the world. There was a four-day air show, too, with aircraft from Canada, Britain and the United States. It included bush planes, World War II fighters, the British Concorde, wing-walkers and ancient biplanes. There was an agricultural show, a water show, a midway, grandstand shows, football games, baseball games, snooker, darts, milk-drinking contests, hula-hoop contests, clowns, music, kite flying, cooking demonstrations, thrill drivers, a lumberjack show, antique cars, art shows and wood carving.

I am taking a law clerk course at college in Edmonton, training to do research for lawyers. At one time I was going to be a lawyer, and I may yet. My parents like the idea of my being a lawyer. What with the dancing and school I don't have a lot of spare time any more. I have a group of friends back home who go bike riding together and to the movies. I read a lot during the school year, but when I'm on the road I don't read anything very important – mostly trash magazines. I'm usually up on who's wearing what, but I don't know who's dying or who shot whom. I read bestsellers like Sidney Sheldon. In school all I read is law.

The Canadian National Exhibition in Toronto runs for twenty days and attracts about 3 million visitors each year.

Facts

Capital city: Ottawa, in the province of Ontario. (Canada does not have a federal district or capital territory.)

Language: Canada is officially a bilingual country – French and English. Those whose mother tongue is English total 14,918,445; mother tongue French, 6,249,095; mother tongue other than French or English, 3,175,640.

Currency: The Canadian dollar is worth 100 cents. At the 1984 exchange rate this works out to 1.76 dollars to the British pound. Coins used in Canada are 1¢, 5¢ (called a nickel), 10¢ (called a dime), 25¢ (called a quarter), 50¢, and $1.

Religion: The religious breakdown of the Canadian population is as follows: Roman Catholic 45 per cent; United Church (combination of Methodist, Presbyterian and others) 20 per cent; Anglican (Church of England in Canada) 13 per cent. Other religions include Greek Orthodox, Lutheran, Hebrew, Continuing Presbyterians, Buddhist, Baha'i and others.

Population: 24,343,180 (1981 census). Of this total 60 per cent of country's people live in a 965-kilometre long strip of countryside from Quebec City to Windsor, Ontario, occupying less than 2 per cent of the total area of Canada. Forty per cent of Canadians are of British origin; 30 per cent are of French origin; then, in order of size, come German, Italian, Dutch, Scandinavian, and Polish. Since World War II 1,000,000 immigrants have come from the United Kingdom, 500,000 from Italy, 250,000 from West Germany, 250,000 from the United States, and many more from a great variety of points of origin. Canada has the largest Icelandic community outside Iceland (Gimli, Manitoba), and during World War II there were more Macdonalds than Smiths in the Canadian Army. The native peoples include 20,000 Inuit (Eskimo) who live within the Arctic Circle, and officially there are 300,000 Indians registered in Canada.

Climate: Canada is a country of extremes. Temperatures range from 60 degrees below zero centigrade to 42 above zero. There are areas classified as cold desert where the snow stays on the ground 12 months a year; there are rain forests on the west coast; there is the North Pole; there are areas as far south as Rome where the weather is balmy; there is the Pacific coast where roses bloom into December.

Geography: Canada is the second largest country in the world. It has an area of 9,976,185 square kilometres (3,851,809 square miles). It covers seven time zones and 1/15 of the land area of the earth. There are 243,791 kilometres (151,489 miles) of coastline. The Great Lakes comprise the largest group of fresh-water lakes in the world. Canada has about 1,609 kilometres (1,000 miles) of flat, wheat-growing plains and mountains over 6,000 metres (19,500 feet) high. There are 482,800 kilometres (300,000 miles) of surfaced roads. To cross mainland Canada by train takes five days and nights.

Government: Canada is a constitutional monarchy. It is made up of 10 provinces and two territories. The provinces, from east to west, are Newfoundland, Nova Scotia, Prince Edward Island, New Brunswick, Quebec, Ontario, Manitoba, Saskatchewan, Alberta and British Columbia. The two territories are the Yukon and the Northwest Territories. Like most Commonwealth countries, Canada's federal Parliament has legislative powers and comprises the Queen (represented by the Governor-General, who is a Canadian), a 282-member House of Commons, and a 104-member Senate. Executive power is vested in the Governor-General, advised by an Executive Council. The main political parties are the Liberals, the Progressive-Conservatives, and the New Democratic party (NDP). Each province has its own government which is autonomous for internal matters such as roads, housing, certain taxes and policing. The provinces have Members of the Provincial Parliament (MPPs) who represent the voting public in the various legislatures. At the municipal level, government is in the hands of elected aldermen and councillors.

Housing: Two-thirds of Canadians live in single, detached dwellings; one-third live in apartments.

Education: Education is a provincial responsibility and, as a result, no common pattern exists. What are known in Canada as public schools are financed by taxation and, within this structure, are free. Non-government-financed schools (called private schools) charge fees. Canada has 67 universities.

Agriculture: Although farming takes place in every province, 79 per cent of Canada's farmland is in the prairies (Manitoba, Saskatchewan and Alberta) and more than half of all farm income is earned in the prairie provinces. Wheat is the crop with the greatest economic value in Canada. Prince Edward

Island and New Brunswick are known for their potato production; Ontario and Quebec are diversified; the prairies produce mostly grain; and British Columbia is a mixed farming area including forestry, dairying and fruit. The four western provinces have most of the ranching. In the early 1900s about 40 per cent of the work force was employed on the farms; today it is more like 12 per cent, mainly because of mechanization.

Industry: Canada is one of the world's leading industrial nations. She is the world's largest producer of zinc and the second largest producer of nickel, potash and asbestos. She is rich in many other minerals, too, but they are often found in the Arctic region where it is difficult to mine economically. Canada also has vast reserves of oil and natural gas. Manufacturing industry employs 25 per cent of the workforce in areas such as motor manufacture, petroleum refining, pulp and paper manufacturing, meat processing and iron and steel. Tourism is also a rapidly growing sector of the economy.

The media: There are 114 daily newspapers, 104 of which print in English, and 10 in French (1983). Weekly, or community, newspapers total more than 1,000. There are approximately 1,000 movie houses (cinemas) and 300 drive-in theatres. In addition to the French and English language newspapers there are about 80 dailies and weeklies which publish in other languages. News services: Canadian Press and United Press International. The broadcasting system combines public and private ownership. The publicly owned Canadian Broadcasting Corporation is designated by law as 'the national broadcasting service', and is also Canada's international broadcaster through shortwave and transcription. CBC owns and operates more than 900 broadcasting stations, transmitters and programme production centres across the country. In addition nearly 400 privately owned or community owned stations and transmitters are associated with CBC as affiliates of its national radio and TV networks. A further 600 privately owned radio and TV stations operate as independent local broadcasters or as part of private commercial networks. CBC Radio is non-commercial. CBC-TV is a combination of commercial and non-commercial services. The private TV networks are CTV with 16 outlets, Global with five, and TVA (French) with nine stations. In addition to the broadcasting stations there are about 500 privately owned cable TV companies.

Glossary

Band (Indian) A division of a tribe; a family group or group of Indians living on a reservation.
Caleche A horse-drawn carriage with a folding top and low wheels.
Caribou A large deer found in the Arctic regions of North America.
Char A trout-like fish found in northern seas and lakes.
Curling A game played on ice in which heavy stones with handles (curling stones or rocks) are slid towards a target.
Hudson's Bay Company An English company chartered in 1670 to trade in all parts of North America drained by rivers which flowed into Hudson Bay.
Inuit The original people of Canada. They are also called Eskimos.
Inuvialuit A group of Inuit who live in the western Arctic region of Canada.
Klondike The area, once famous for the gold rush, around the Klondike River in Canada's Yukon Territory.
Midway A place in a fair where sideshows are located.
Mukluk A soft boot worn by the Inuit. It is usually made of sealskin.
Pennsylvania Dutch A group of German-speaking people who live in east Pennsylvania. They are descended from an eighteenth-century group of settlers from south-west Germany and Switzerland.
Silt The deposit of mud or clay usually found at the bottom of a river or lake.
Sous chef A chef who is second in command to the head chef. His main responsibility is for making sauces.
Spigot A tap which may be driven into a tree to extract the sap.
Trapline A line of traps through a designated area in which one person may trap for animals.
Whipcord A strong worsted or cotton fabric with a ribbed surface.
Whitewater A stretch of rapids on a river where the water has a white, foamy surface.

Index

Agriculture 41, 58
   Dairy farming 32
   Potatoes 38
   Wheat 16–17
Alberta 30, 56
Algonquin Park 28–9

Bears 28, 29
British Columbia 42

Canadian Broadcasting Corporation 54–5
Canadian National Exhibition 56–7
Canadian Pacific Railway 14–15, 30–31
Canadian Shield 22–3
Climate 1, 11, 41, 58
Copper 15, 23, 38, 39

Economy, the 35
Edmonton 31, 56
Education 58
   Colleges 27
   Schools 33, 52–3
Eskimos *see* Inuit

Fishing 34
   Lobster fishing 20–21
Food 44–5
Fur trade 6, 10, 25

Gas 30–31
Girl Guides 33
Gold 11, 23, 41
Government 58
   and the Inuit 9
Great Lakes 19

Halifax 21
History 14–15, 24–5, 34–5, 46
Hudson Bay 22
Hudson's Bay Company 8, 14
Hurons 24–5

Ice age 34
Immigrants 15, 21, 26
Indians 10, 12, 24, 25, 37, 41, 50–51
Industry 34, 42, 46, 52, 59
   Fishing 34
   Gas 30–31
   Lobster fishing 20–21
   Logging 42–3
   Mining 38–9
   Oil 30–31
Inuit 8–9
Inuvialuit 8–9

Jesuits 24–5

Klondike 11

Language 47, 58
Lobster fishing 20–21
Logging 42–3

Media 26–7, 54–5, 59
Minerals 23, 38–9
Mining 38–9
Missionaries 24–5
Moose 28, 29
Mounties *see* Royal Canadian Mounted Police

National Parks 28, 45
Newfoundland 34–5
Niagara Escarpment 13, 19
Niagara Falls 12–13, 19
Niagara River 12, 13, 25
Nickel 15, 23, 38, 39
North-West Mounted Police 41
Nova Scotia 20–21

Oil 30–31
Ottawa 6, 35
Ottawa River 6–7, 25

Politics 29

Pollution 29
Population 1, 49, 58
Prairies 16, 37, 58
Prince Edward Island 38

Quebec City 46–7

Railroads 14–15
Rocky Mountains 1, 15, 30, 31, 44–5
Royal Canadian Mounted Police 40–41

St. Lawrence Seaway 18, 19
Ste. Marie Among the Hurons 24–5
Settlers 24–5
Sport
   Curling 23
   Football 36–7
   Inuit sports 9
   Skiing 45, 52
Superior, Lake 19

Toronto 26–7
Tourism 13, 22, 26–7, 44–5, 52
Transport
   Air 48–9
   Railroad 14–15
Trapping 10

Wildlife 17, 28–9

Yukon 40–41

Acknowledgements

All the photographs in this book were supplied by the author with the exception of the following: Canadian Department of Regional Industrial Expansion 29, 34; Canadian High Commission 17, 21, 23 (top), 31, 35, 46; CPAir 48, CPHotels 45; CPRail 15; Department of Indian Affairs 51; Government of Nova Scotia 20; INCO 39; Ontario Ministry of Tourism and Recreation 19; Irwin Patterson 57; Greg Smith 6 (both), 7; Wilderness Tours (Hugh Mackenzie) 8 (both) 9.